EMPOWERED
2022

WORDS TO LIBERATE

Edited By Jenni Harrison

First published in Great Britain in 2022 by:

Young Writers
Remus House
Coltsfoot Drive
Peterborough
PE2 9BF
Telephone: 01733 890066
Website: www.youngwriters.co.uk

All Rights Reserved
Book Design by Ashley Janson
© Copyright Contributors 2022
Softback ISBN 978-1-83928-656-8

Printed and bound in the UK by BookPrintingUK
Website: www.bookprintinguk.com
YB0520F

⭐ FOREWORD ⭐

Since 1991, here at Young Writers we have celebrated the awesome power of creative writing, especially in young adults where it can serve as a vital method of expressing their emotions and views about the world around them. In every poem we see the effort and thought that each student published in this book has put into their work and by creating this anthology we hope to encourage them further with the ultimate goal of sparking a life-long love of writing.

Our latest competition for secondary school students, Empowered, challenged young writers to consider what was important to them. We wanted to give them a voice, the chance to express themselves freely and honestly, something which is so important for these young adults to feel confident and listened to. They could give an opinion, share a memory, consider a dilemma, impart advice or simply write about something they love. There were no restrictions on style or subject so you will find an anthology brimming with a variety of poetic styles and topics. We hope you find it as absorbing as we have.

We encourage young writers to express themselves and address subjects that matter to them, which sometimes means writing about sensitive or contentious topics. If you have been affected by any issues raised in this book, details on where to find help can be found at
www.youngwriters.co.uk/info/other/contact-lines

★ CONTENTS ★

Harris Academy Merton, Mitcham

Eric Ramakrishnan (12)	1
Saadhana Swamiappan (14)	2
Lamaat Mirza (12)	3
Sereena Wedderburn (13)	4

King's Academy, Ringmer

Ella McPherson-Avery (12)	5
Jack Powell (11)	6
Devon-Danielle Booker (14)	8
Lily Burgan (12)	10
Kai Kenechukwu Onyeka (12)	12
Samuel Chrismas (12)	14
Max Willis (13)	16
Anni Crane (12)	18
Emma Bartlett (14)	20
Isaac Tatlow (12)	21
Florence Mackmin (12)	22
Orlah-Daisy Jones (12)	24
Lillie Bourne (13)	25
Betsy Wheatley (12)	26
Rachel Curran (13)	28
Bruce Thomas (12)	29
Elsa Johnson-Gregory (12)	30
Molly Sudan (12)	32
Josh Naylor (11)	33
Tionne Andrew (13)	34
Elliot Porter (12)	35
Abigayle Fleet (14)	36
Amelia Wheatley (12)	37
Dexter Eglese-Coy (12)	38
Callie Peacock (14)	39
Scarlett Taylor (13)	40
Evie Hyne (13)	41
Harry Bull (12)	42
Isaac Cottingham (12)	43
Theo Eremin (13)	44
Isaac Harley (14)	45
Jessica Lucas (11)	46
Olivia Woolley (12)	47
Zachary Linstrem (12)	48
Arthur Salisbury (14)	49
Fionn Kiersey-Green (14)	50
Joseph Donald (11)	51
Mary Sunguro (14)	52
Daisy Salisbury (12)	53
Jack Merry (11)	54
Rudy Wilson (13)	55
Alex Went (13)	56
Joshua Marchant (14)	57
Finlay Shaw (12)	58
Maisey Dodd	59
Abi Teague (11)	60
Hannah Price (12)	61
Jessica Standen (12)	62
Gabriella Rossi (12)	63
Rory Lynch (12)	64
Lloyd Thomas (12)	65
Poppy Taranczuk	66
Jessica Frizzell (12)	67
Elliott Luscombe (12)	68
Callum Rickard (12)	69
Ollie Smith (12)	70
Isaac Parker (12)	71
Ben Griffin (12)	72

Nunnery Wood High School, Worcester

Rebecca Sonusi (14)	73
Julia Pieczara (14)	74
Izzie Faull (12)	77
Josh Ruane (14)	78
Isabelle Mann (14)	80
Dhyan Krishna Binu (12)	82
Sarah Goodman (13)	83
Amy Farrow (14)	84
Alfie Thompson (14)	86
Emily Kirkland (14)	88
Tia Agyemam (13)	90
Amy Evans (12)	91
Edward (12)	92
Amy Mills (13)	93
Tom Nockton (12)	94
Joe Murphy (14)	96
Shieanne Corpuz (13)	97
Alex Donello (12)	98
Angel Fortey (13)	99
Lara Jackson (12)	100
Kamil Kobylarz (14)	101
Kristina Neale (12)	102
Molly Tyrrell (14)	103
Lacey Taylor (12)	104
James Vianello (11)	105
Jack Tomboline (11)	106
Nathan Rhodes (12)	107
Harry Bloss (12)	108
Jack Edwards (12)	109
Ruby Scarrott (13)	110
Lilly Humphries (12)	111
Jess Holmes (13)	112
Maia Pop (13)	113
Dan Turculet (12)	114
Zoya Ali (12)	115
Kaiden Godding (13)	116
Maroosh Akhtar (11)	117
Oliver Cartwright (12)	118
Evangeline Dowtin (13)	119
Lucas Sones (12)	120
Matthew Blaikie (14)	121
Maliakah Arshad-Mehmood (13)	122
Tom Brown (14)	123
Dion Cartwright (13)	124
Archie Burton (12)	125
Summer Drummond (11)	126
Antoinette Thea Ragasa (13)	127
Harvey Symonds (12)	128
Ayesha Tabassum (13)	129
James Barratt (12)	130
Monty Simpson (13)	131
Gracie Lee (12)	132
Jessica Cattermole (11)	133
Steven Evans (14)	134
Salma Sherif (11)	135
Macy Holder (14)	136
Amelia Ali (12)	137
Callum Bannister (13)	138
Cerys Jones (14)	139
Oliver Leonard (12)	140
Ben Schaus (12)	141
Charlie Bunce (12)	142
Aleena Ilyas (14)	143
Sam Jennings (12)	144
Georgia Grooms (11)	145
Evie Kirkland (12)	146
Lincoln Atkins (12)	147
Harry Davies (13)	148
Tanisha Parrott (12)	149
Thomas Walters (13)	150
Siddhant Dubey (13)	151
Mikayeel Akbar (12)	152
Thea Fieldhouse (12)	153
Emily Franklin (12)	154

RGS Worcester, Upper Tything

Anya Wood	155
Issy Pottinger (13)	156
Eva Wilson-Thomas (12)	157

St Andrew The Apostle School, London

Daisy Hossack (13)	158
Christiana Christofi (12)	159
Katina Georgiou	160
Michael Georgiou (12)	161
Ana Halliday	162
Sahana Goonasekera	163
Stefan Kousoulou	164

Trinity Academy Leeds, Leeds

Jeremiel Mbogol (12)	165
Moram Osman (12)	166
Abigail Kidane (12)	168
Mustafa Goulami (11)	170
Tasnim Mohammed (12)	171
Laaibah Hussain (12)	172
Amina Almjadami (12)	173
Deyana Ismail (12)	174
Jaromira Stejckova (12)	175
Ansh Minhas (12)	176
Uali Binium (12)	177
Athelia Duberry (11)	178
Ryan Adam (12)	179
Jasmine Fielding (12)	180
Nicole Bazenova (12)	181
Chloe Elysse Carag (12)	182

THE POEMS

Nature Is A Beauty

A myriad of colours over the horizon.
Hues of orange, red and yellow glisten the sky
With a radiant promise of what is to come.
Birds appear and then vanish as they flutter by.

The arrival of the morning is imminent
With the sounds of the world awakening from its slumber.
Adults and children greet the new day they've been sent
And look upon the world with a sense of wonder.

It is a world that has started anew
With jaw-dropping things that nature has to offer
Is very much a few.

Looking at all of the deadly mountains,
The tip of the mountain is like a gigantic spearhead
It's the type that reminds you of the huge hostile fountains
Enormous peaks like arrowheads.

They caught sight of the sea far below.
The sea around the island is a shimmering blue,
Reflecting all the colours of the rainbow
As beautiful dolphins swim right through.

Eric Ramakrishnan (12)
Harris Academy Merton, Mitcham

Golden Hour

Yellow rays break through these clouds
Like the tide reaching the shore.
The dark of the night is shadowed by light,
Mistakes are lost to the day before.

This is the blue, the purple, the grey.
These are the clouds that are white.
This is the slow rotation of Earth
That changes the scene in the sky.

This is the lazy afternoon,
The magnificent golden hour.
Alone as the light falls in waves on the blinds.
Orange, the colour of power.

The lonely night with the stars,
White streaks of headlights speeding past.
Sound asleep are their beautiful souls,
While yours has never felt more alive.

A wonderful world
And a wonderful life.

Saadhana Swamiappan (14)
Harris Academy Merton, Mitcham

Lungs Of The Earth

I think that I shall never sea
Anything as beautiful as a tree.

Tree bark is the brown fingerprints of my soul,
For as I touch it I feel as if I have accomplished my goal.

The one tree that looks up at God all day,
Will always lift its arms, it is now time to pray.

The tree that may in summer wear
A family of robins in her hair.

Trees are here every day
Where we can go out to play.

Poems are made by people like me,
But only God can make a one-of-a-kind tree.

Lamaat Mirza (12)
Harris Academy Merton, Mitcham

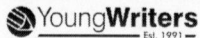

Why Me?

Be proud of who you are,
But how could I ever be,
When they tell you being black
Is nothing but a race.

They touch my hair and judge,
They call me names,
They don't care about my ancestors,
Or learn where Jamaica is.

When Dave says "Black is beautiful" he is right,
Proud of Rosa Parks for putting up a fight.
Serena Williams setting the standards high,
Maybe they should learn some manners.

Sereena Wedderburn (13)
Harris Academy Merton, Mitcham

Just One More Day

Just one more day
Just one more day of having to fit in
So you don't get bullied by the popular kids
Just one more day of having to get up every morning
With a smile on your face even when you're at your lowest
Just one more day of having to cover your face
With enough make-up to be 'pretty enough' to hang out with somebody
Just one more day of not being able to breathe
Just so you can fit into the tiny school skirts
Because everyone knows you need to wear the smallest size to be popular
Just one more day of having to watch what you say
Because otherwise the popular kids will judge you, bully you
And pick on you for the rest of your life
Just one more day
The three words
We have to tell ourselves each morning just to get out of bed
Just one more day of telling ourselves that things get better in the end
Until you realise that it isn't just one more day
It is forever
P.S. you are amazing even if you aren't popular!

Ella McPherson-Avery (12)
King's Academy, Ringmer

The Future We All Climb Together

La collina - the wonder like heaven
Xiǎoshān - we must climb it all as one
Pahaadee - it is as difficult as breaking a diamond in half
Pahorb - and at the top is where we are all meant to be
Buurta - but we must help each other
Die koppie - and respect everything around and on it
Kholm - we must no longer knock each other down
Eondeog - instead we must leave all hatred and slavery behind, get past our differences
Altall - and work together to make it to the top and beyond
'O ka pu'u - we must prove that we can work with nature
Bakken - and put others before ourselves
Blury - we must flourish as a beautiful flower, not as a weed
Der Hügel - the I must not be separate from the other, do not judge people because they are different
O lófos, - we must understand that nature is not all ours for the taking
Oka - we must understand that things can be different or we shall never succeed
Bukit - and that we cannot continue to destroy here or out there
An cnoc - we must all unite with each other and nature
Ti mòn lan - and make ourselves peaceful
Hóllinn - in order to not cut our journey short

Kopec - we must respect each other and the other
Y bryn - our beliefs, differences and opinions shall be accepted, celebrated and not just simply put aside
The hill - the hikers must stick together
It may not seem as difficult as a mountain
But that doesn't mean that it is not hard
And that we should therefore not try
It seems small, but it's easy to get lost on the way
If we continue to fight amongst ourselves
We will never be worthy to discover what is out there
I am me, you are you
But that cannot stop us from all climbing the hill
Unless we allow it to
It would be pointless and unwise to stop each other
We are not significant unless we come together and make peace with what is.

Jack Powell (11)
King's Academy, Ringmer

The Real Me

I look at the screen,
I wish I looked like them:
Their glamorous hair,
Their eyes that sparkle like a gem.
I look in the mirror,
From my eye there's a tear,
I'm ugly, I'm worthless, I'm queer.
I look at the ground,
I don't want people to see,
If they see this mess,
They'll make fun of me.

Behind their screen there's a filter,
Their hair is not real,
I start to realise,
I need time to heal.
Their eyes are not gems,
It's just an editing effect,
I start to realise,
It's myself I need to accept.
I look in the mirror,
A smile lights up my face,
Everyone's different,
Beauty isn't a race.
I look up and smile,
And people smile back,

I start to realise it was my confidence
That I used to lack.

Beauty doesn't require a certain gender or race,
I start to allow myself to go at a steady pace.
I start to let go of the negativity
I breathe in and out,
And I set them all free.
I replace what was once a sad and lonely place,
And fill up my mind with positivity;
For now I no longer feel so melancholy,
I have rid myself of depression and anxiety,
I no longer shadow myself;
I let the world see the real me.

Devon-Danielle Booker (14)
King's Academy, Ringmer

Body Power

Do you love yourself?
No.
Do you love your body?
No, why?
Too skinny, too fat
Even just a bit too tall
Nah, that's just who you're meant to be

Just 'cause of how those Insta girls look
Oh so you're plus size, go wear that cute bikini
All those people online are an illusion
You have spots? They do too
It's just make-up. It's just a filter.

Go out, but out loud, be proud
Be a big fat wow queen
If you have a vision, a mind, a voice
And some love you can do anything
Honestly.
Imagine the world if everyone looked the same
It would be so dull and plain
So don't hold yourself into this slim curvy figure
If you already have something so unique.

Just think of a snowflake
You'll never find two snowflakes that look the same

As they're all so intricately formed.
We are all snowflakes.

Just because a person is a bit bigger
Or a bit skinnier, taller or shorter
Doesn't make them ugly or a freak,
They are just as much of a person that you'll ever meet.
The labels given to you can't define you, only your actions can.
Don't ever think you'll never be that girl
Living in a Barbie world.

Lily Burgan (12)
King's Academy, Ringmer

Spoken Words

If I was white would it change me for who I am?
If I was white would I still have my history in my Igbo name?
Why is being white superior when white is just a label?
Skin colour represents who our ancestors are and our history.
Not for who is superior and who isn't.
Are we able to live in our own skin with being discriminated against?
Are we able to breathe without being watched like prey from afar?
Are we able to walk home without turning our backs to see if we're being watched?
It has never stopped.
Again, again and again like a train on tracks.
But when will we turn the page to start a new chapter?
But when will racism end, causing so many lives to end so soon?
But when will people stop saying black people are bad and so on?
But when will the world change?
Black people may be a community,
White people may be a community,
But humans are what makes the world.
So why hate your fellow human because of their skin colour?
When a leopard isn't going to hate another leopard for having another spot?

The world needs to change for the better.
Change is needed for world peace.
We all need to start changing.
This time for equality.
So I demand that racism needs to end.

Kai Kenechukwu Onyeka (12)
King's Academy, Ringmer

It's Up To Us

I look up at the sky
The heat of a greenhouse world
Global warming, poor penguins die
There won't be any ice at all
Why they do this makes me want to cry
But all they do is stall
I want to think that it's not so bad, it's not so bad

Lots of ice and polar bears but they'll be dead next year
For so many helpless animals the end really is near
But the important people of the world don't care for the atmosphere
If you try to talk to them they'll act like they can't hear
Looking away, closing their eyes and blocking their ears
Just so they can afford a big shiny chandelier
The people have the Earth in our hands
And stab it with a spear
And just the thought of it brings me to tears.

And then I realise that it's up to us
They take our world and throw it under the bus
And just as we thought we had been defeated by the greenhouse gases
And the way that we've been treated
We start to see a shining light of hope
To save our planet all broken and asleep

The Earth is on the minds of a billion young people
To save the Earth from all things bad or evil.

Samuel Chrismas (12)
King's Academy, Ringmer

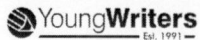

A Woman's World

It's a woman's choice
Until a man decides it isn't
Until women have to stay silent
Until we have to become compliant

It's a woman's body
Until a man takes control
Until women have to play a role
Until we have goals

It's a woman's progress
Until a man takes all the credit
Until it was a woman who said it
Until we are seen as unfit

It's a woman's life
Until a man doesn't wait for permission
Until women meet competition
Until we have to follow tradition

It's a woman's strength
Until a man takes her power
Until women are seen as a delicate flower
Until we are forced to cower

It's a women's clothing
Until a man tells her what to wear

Until women are seen as too bare
Until we have to beware

It's a woman's sexuality
Until a man thinks he can change her
Until women are sexualised and called slurs
Until we are looked down upon as bitter

It's a woman's right
Until a man makes a law
Until the women saw
We really have no rights at all.

Max Willis (13)
King's Academy, Ringmer

Be Empowered To Make A Change

The world is dying
Nature is crying
The situation is grave
There is going to be no planet to save
The ice caps are melting away
Our world is turning from green to grey

We need to come out the dark
And follow the spark
Which will empower us to say
That we need to act today

Give a voice to the weak
So they can speak
About the planet that protected us for so long
And that nature is light and pollution is wrong

Then that one quiet speech that you gave to a crowd
Is now a message and it's ringing loud
You can empower people to make a change
You taught them that standing up for their world isn't strange

It takes one person to change a world for good
You definitely could
Let the world empower you

Be part of a crew
Which steers the Earth the right way
The time for a better world is today.

Anni Crane (12)
King's Academy, Ringmer

Equality

Doing the same job for much less pay,
Good enough for centre stage but pushed back out of the way.
Being in a minority in this world it's just not fair;
Something's got to give.

Misogyny at your work or down the street,
Overlooked for promotion unless he thinks you're 'sweet'.
Being female in a man's world it's just not fair;
Something's got to give.

Unable to board a train or bus
Without creating a dreadful fuss.
Being disabled in a busy world it's just not fair;
Something's got to give.

Putting up with tuts and stares
From others who judge without any cares.
Being different in this world it's just not fair;
Something's got to give.

This world is full of so much good
In every town and neighbourhood.
It doesn't have to be unfair;
But something's got to give.

Emma Bartlett (14)
King's Academy, Ringmer

Lucky Socks

My brother plays football
He is rather good
He is the master of the field
Lethal legs, smashing goals and kicks that kill
When I asked him the secret of his skill
He said, "Truth be told,
It's the empowerment of my lucky socks."

The day of the maths test came very quick
My mind went blank, I really did feel sick.
Like a miracle, it came to me
To make my maths brain truly rock,
I needed to borrow those lucky socks.

While he slept, in I crept
Those lucky socks were mine to get.
Lying on his treasure box
I spied the lucky socks.
As I reached out to claim my prize
A smell so bad, it hit me by surprise!
I ran back out in a hurry
It smelt as bad as week-old curry.
My maths test was no longer a worry
Because lucky socks weren't for me
As I can be empowered...

By believing in myself.

Isaac Tatlow (12)
King's Academy, Ringmer

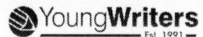

You Are You And There Is Nothing Anyone Can Do About It

You are free
You are proud
You will do things differently
You will do things that aren't allowed
Break away the chains
No holding back
Take hold of the reigns
It is you that they lack
You are you and there is nothing anyone can do about it

Be strong
Be kind
If you are everyone else will follow along
Don't fight your instincts but use your mind
You are you and there is nothing anyone can do about it

Every time you speak you risk being drowned
However, you must rise above it
Make a sound
For you can change the world even just a bit
You are you and there is nothing anyone can do about it

Fight to rise from your ashes
Fight to be who you are
It doesn't matter if your life is in stashes
Remember that you are a star
You are you and there is nothing anyone can do about it.

Florence Mackmin (12)
King's Academy, Ringmer

Not My Fault

Not my fault my legs are distracting you
I don't need to cover up, you need to grow up
Not my fault my body isn't perfect enough for you
Not my fault you don't like how my make-up looks
I did it for myself, not you
Not my fault you think I'm 'moody'
And no, it's not 'that time of the month'
Not my fault my legs are too hairy
Not my fault you don't like how much I cry
Not my fault he bullies me
Of course he doesn't 'fancy me'
Because 'boys will be boys' you say
Not my fault you think I'm 'emo' for being sad
Not my fault I'm not perfect enough for your 'standards'
Your unrealistic standards for a teenage girl, like me
I'm only a young girl after all
Too much pressure to look perfect
My poem makes you 'uncomfortable'?
Not my fault.

Orlah-Daisy Jones (12)
King's Academy, Ringmer

Let Me Not Be Beautiful

You know what compliment I am so sick of hearing?
"You're beautiful."
As if my worth is belittled into how my face is shaped
The slope of my nose, the fullness of my lips.
I am sick of being told I am 'pretty'
As if it is a trade-off with being intelligent
I know I am smart and funny and kind-hearted
So compliment me on that
On something I believe, something I know is real
I am sick of being complimented on some strange abstract society norm
It will not reassure me
It will not make me love myself
I am so sick of how meaningless the word 'beauty' has become
It is not true
I do not want it to be true
I am content as the funny friend
The smart girl in the back of the classroom
Let me be that
Just let me not be beautiful.

Lillie Bourne (13)
King's Academy, Ringmer

Miracle In The Making

The tiniest feet we've ever seen,
Hands as fragile as a broken wing.
Fear envelops our soul,
Unable to take control.
Our miracle in the making.

A delicate stalk,
We embrace this fearsome walk.
Born too soon,
Our belief strengthens through each new moon.
Our miracle in the making.

The angels worked hard day and night,
Helping you through your daily fight.
The wires that flood you are there to protect you.
Our miracle in the making.

The buds you show,
Are a sign you are ready to grow.
We must have hope
Our miracle in the making.
It's our only way to cope.
The tears of joy,
A family we are,
Home at last,
You have come so far

A beautifully bloomed flower
Standing proud for all the see
Forever you will be...
Our miracle in the making.

Betsy Wheatley (12)
King's Academy, Ringmer

Now

Now
I am alive now

I feel my heartbeat again
I feel it race, but this time it feels good
It is strong and invigorating, not like usual
This is not like usual

I am alive now

I feel the wind on my skin again
I feel the coolness of the air on my arms, in my lungs
I am light and I am breathing, not like usual
This is not like usual

This is loud music in the kitchen
This is bike rides in the sun
This is laughing in the pouring rain
This is dancing to old songs
I am alive

This moment will end
But for the promise of another moment like this
I won't give up on myself until the next one comes
Like usual.

Rachel Curran (13)
King's Academy, Ringmer

The Earth

The Earth: the world that gave us everything
The world that made us what we are today
Without it we have nothing
With it, we have logic, ethicality and understanding
It is our world
A place that has waited for 50 million lifetimes to see us
Insignificant dots in the vastness of the universe
It is like the tranquil oasis at the centre of the barren, hostile, inhospitable wasteland
Home to everything we have
More organisms, environments, worlds
Than we can imagine
It is a place that has given us innumerable resources
A world we should preserve and protect
A world ten thousand times older than humanity
A world we can rely upon
If we maintain it correctly.

Bruce Thomas (12)
King's Academy, Ringmer

The Dance Of Today

Caught by the shouting
Taken by the calling
The women that we love
Hope is dying

Caught by society
Taken by looks
The world that we loved
Confidence isn't rising

You've got to believe
But it's taken by those whose words disgust you
A tsunami of hate

Feeling empowered
A crime
The inequality is rising
The world is dividing

Now stand up for yourself
Ricochet the words who may think
You don't belong
But you do

Fight the feeling
Not them
Who may think you're not
Special

Wonderful
Magical
The dance of today.

Elsa Johnson-Gregory (12)
King's Academy, Ringmer

Be Unique, It's Not Good To Follow The Crowd

See, although things can be tough
And life can be rough
When you follow the crowd
Your personalities and unique ideas go behind the cloud.

Imagine life where everybody was the same
You can't proclaim
Life would be lame
But imagine if we were all different
Life would be magnificent
You could have your own ideas
You could have your own fears
You could think what you wanted to think
Blink when you wanted to blink
You could be independent
Your ideas would be transcendent
You would be recognised for the amazing things you've done
And would stand out brighter than the sun.

Molly Sudan (12)
King's Academy, Ringmer

My Cat

My cat is black, like water in the night
Black like a pirate's beard
Black like a dark pearl
His meow is like the devil going to Heaven
My cat is like the midnight sky
His whole being is as dark as a void
His coat is silky smooth like velvet
His eyes are green, like freshly mowed grass
His whiskers are long, like fine cotton thread
His nose is wet, like a puddle on the ground
He resembles my everything.

I will let him sleep
With my hands I shall feed him
Let the others run free
The food belongs to my cat
Eat my cat, for I am here
To feed you, my dear.

Josh Naylor (11)
King's Academy, Ringmer

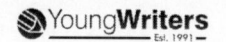

A Disintegrating Future

You have stolen my future with your careless, thoughtless, selfish actions
Just to suit your satisfaction
As different biomes are attacked, animals are forced to suffer
Now they are forced to adapt in order to make them tougher.

Because of you, it is up to my generation
To try to fix this world with multiple creations
For if we don't there is no Planet B
For us to be happily free.

This is an emergency, time is running out,
We need to hurry, have no doubt
With timed threats to species, protection is vital
If we don't save them now, extinction will be their title.

Tionne Andrew (13)
King's Academy, Ringmer

Champions

Composure is key
To complete a task that's been set
Let our minds foresee
Visualise the ball in their net

This is our game
Be determined, don't be fooled
Let everyone know our name
"Ringmer Sunday let's take it all"

A last-minute attack
Could this be the decider?
The ref glances at his watch
A goal from our striker

A message to all
Don't be sad, don't fall
Just put your mind to it
And push, push through it

Do you want to know why?
'Cause here's a good secret
Anything is possible!

Elliot Porter (12)
King's Academy, Ringmer

Our Bodies, Our Choices

How would you feel if your body was taken?
I'm not just metaphorically speaking.
Being taken away with no sign or warning,
You have it today and don't the next morning.

Your body is shaking as you lie down at night.
You cover the scars
But you can't end the fight.

Now imagine the hurt, the dread, the pain.
Your uterus covered in your abuser's name.

You have no choice to escape from this game,
For men have the right and we have the blame.

This is our life, our body, our choices,
This will not be the end of hearing our voices.

Abigayle Fleet (14)
King's Academy, Ringmer

Empowerment

Living beyond feelings
To continue no matter what
Dancing in the rain
And to smile when all you feel is pain
It is what takes you far beyond yesterday
And into the presence of tomorrow
To engage you in the moment, to distract you from sorrow

Empowerment is found deep within the soul
Understanding to embrace it is an ever-learning goal

A promise to empower others in any way we can
For spirits to be lifted
For kindness to be gifted
Accepting with gratitude and paying it forward
We will empower others
We give you our word
Empowerment.

Amelia Wheatley (12)
King's Academy, Ringmer

Rights For Climate Change

My future self is to have the power against climate change
Able to stop deforestation and over-fishing with a force to get behind
I will gather a group and make a stop to all of this
It doesn't matter who you are or what you look like
You have the power over this
So come on together and we can make these rights come true
It's all in your self of what we can do
But if we don't start now then it's too late
And there will be nothing but buildings everywhere
And no nature or fish in the sea
Also icebergs will melt from too much heat like snow in summer.

Dexter Eglese-Coy (12)
King's Academy, Ringmer

Her

Every morning, she wakes at an early hour
Every morning, she sacrifices the chance of a shower
Every morning, she inspires those around her
Every morning, she provides the warmth of a lover
Incomprehensible, her motivation confuses me
How does a person continue relentlessly
Through the screams, nags, fights and whines
She keeps her head high with a smile that shines
No matter the happening
Her love is unmatching
"Who inspires you?"
They ask as if my answer is new
It will always and forever be
The woman empowered next to me
Her.

Callie Peacock (14)
King's Academy, Ringmer

I'm Not Like You

I shouldn't have to be just like you
To do the things that I want to do
I shouldn't have to just pretend
To be happy all the time - this has to end!

I shouldn't have to copy and paste
My personality - it seems such a waste
I don't want to end up like you
So I'm gonna do the things that I want to do!

I'll be myself; I won't depend
On rude, insensitive, ill-mannered 'friends'
So when you're lost and unable to see
I'll smile and I'll think, *I'm glad that's not me.*

Scarlett Taylor (13)
King's Academy, Ringmer

Change

We all have a choice
That's what they say
Tell that to the kids
Who had to work every day

We all have a voice
That's what they say
Tell that to the people
Who lived under a tyrant's reign

We all have rights
That's what they say
Tell that to the women
Who had to fight every day

We are unstoppable
That's what they say
Tell that to us
Just two years ago today

The world is changing
No day is the same
Our history is the one thing
That will never change.

Evie Hyne (13)
King's Academy, Ringmer

Black

No matter who you are
No matter where you come from
No matter
No matter
You are who you are
You can not change but you can think
You can because you are you
No matter what people say
No matter if you are good enough
You can practise because you can get better
No matter what colour skin you have
No matter
No matter
Because black is good
Black is wonderful
Put your hand on mine
Nothing wrong with that because black is good
And we are all the same
We are a community.

Harry Bull (12)
King's Academy, Ringmer

The Plane

The missile curved and shot the plane
It chipped and lifted then nose-dived again
The pilot struggled to regain control
Fought with all his might against the downward pull

What happened? Why? We were all fine
The sky was clear, no stars about
Passengers screamed and cried and prayed
The plane was slipping from the air.

Innocent people about their business
Families excited for the holidays abroad
Unknown to them the countries they crossed
Were at war below them and this was the cost.

Isaac Cottingham (12)
King's Academy, Ringmer

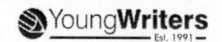

Tyrants Are Supreme But I Am Free

They control me and order me,
But they do not own me,
My blood lost for their cause,
But my life I lost for myself.

They sit and wait,
While we take,
I kill and die,
While they dine.

Tears shed,
For loved ones,
Who will never return,
From the dark secrets of war.

This is war,
We could have avoided,
But now it's too late,
For we are left to die.

But that's fine,
Because from this,
We can create something beautiful,
Peace.

Theo Eremin (13)
King's Academy, Ringmer

Life

Life is difficult
It's meant to be
Yet it's not right
To treat the different differently
You need to be bright
And open your eyes
Take in the differences
Breathe out the hate
Think about your views
Talk to your mate
About the differences
About the fact that
Life is difficult
It's meant to be
Yet it's not right
To take out your difficulty
On the people who are different
How would you feel
If we treated everyone like equals?

Isaac Harley (14)
King's Academy, Ringmer

Peace Of Mind

Arm in arm these countries parade
In a contract they have made
Now an oblivion in Putin's head
Which concludes lots of Ukrainians dead
Though Zelenskyy's country is oh so small
They all stand graciously tall
Russia biggest out of all
Is left with hatred and popularity miniscule
Hypnotised by Vladimir's words
Russian brains are splitting into thirds
United countries stand for Ukraine
Praying that Putin will end this game
Ukraine we stand with you!

Jessica Lucas (11)
King's Academy, Ringmer

Broken

Ruins of wither and crumble
Broken fans gaze at broken streets and houses
Even the sunshine feels like burning rain
A never-ending lonely game

Soldiers strive onwards, thinking of home
Parents holding children close
Wishing they could tell them they're all fine
Without maybe having to lie

But hopes and legends never die
Or shatter or break or fade
It's the time to act, to open the world's eye
And together we can make them see.

Olivia Woolley (12)
King's Academy, Ringmer

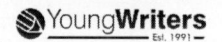

The Crazy Dog

My dog is as crazy as a chimpanzee
My dog is as calm as a house cat
He is as hyper as a cheetah
Or as chilled as a koala
My dog has the energy of lightning
My dog is as inactive as a sloth
My dog represents happiness

I will comfort him in his bed
With my tennis ball I will play with him
With dog biscuits I feed him
Let my enemies walk their dogs on the road
The fields are for me and my dog
Play, my dog, while I throw you your ball.

Zachary Linstrem (12)
King's Academy, Ringmer

Blind Voice

It really doesn't matter what you say
Because when your voice is blind
What comes out your lips may
As well be written by another mind

Those who talk without seeing clearly
Are as bad as those who deceive sincerely

But those who talk in faith
They will be the ones to shape the future
And free the speechless of the wraith
Who ties up injustice with lies like a suture

So to talk is to give
But to mean is to live.

Arthur Salisbury (14)
King's Academy, Ringmer

A United Europe

Once a year Europe comes together
To celebrate music
Countries we never hear about enter
We get a taste from 40-43 different nationalities.

We listen to intense voting of nations
Giving points to one another
Like Greece giving points to Cyprus

Then in May 2022 Turin, Italy
Love, solidarity and support at the Eurovision Song Contest
Giving Ukraine their win
So I give douze point à l'humanite.

Fionn Kiersey-Green (14)
King's Academy, Ringmer

Just Try

Even if you're feeling down
You should always give it a try
Even if you know you probably won't get what you want
Just try,
I'm writing this for the £100 award
I probably won't win and at first I didn't really want to
But I just tried
And now I've got my hopes up
I'm almost finished now
Thinking about what I would do with the money
Probably won't get it but
I just tried.

Joseph Donald (11)
King's Academy, Ringmer

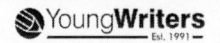

I Look Into The Mirror

Mirror, mirror on the wall
You're my favourite thing of all
Not because I'm vain
Or that my reflection twinkles
Back at me like a star in a river
But because you show me the real reality
The facade that shines on top of the raw me
The mirror that turns insecurities into beauties and makes me happy
The mirror that teaches me to love me
Mirror mirror on the wall
This is why I'll love you forever more.

Mary Sunguro (14)
King's Academy, Ringmer

Do They?

Do they tarnish your fame?
Do they call you names?
Or mock the one you already own?
Do they ensure only your weaknesses are shown?
And even worse, convince you they're right?
Remember, it's only through spite
So don't give in, continue to fight

Do they harden your heart?
Do they rip it apart?
Keep your head high
Aim for the sky
Accept that you are different
It makes you magnificent.

Daisy Salisbury (12)
King's Academy, Ringmer

Ringmer Rovers Is My Team

Ringmer Rovers is my team
To win the league was our dream
Hitting ultimate highs and lows
And cheering when the whistle blows!

Supporting my team playing in defence
Our passion, it's no pretence
We pass and move when on the field
Protecting the goal like we are a shield

During that final game
When our glory came
Finishing top of the table
We had proved ourselves able!

Jack Merry (11)
King's Academy, Ringmer

Power Of Friends

My friends are the family I got to choose
Take a chance on a friend
What have you got to lose?

Yesterday, today, tomorrow and after
Friends fill my day with wicked laughter

I'm the eldest brother and a thoughtful son
But with friends I feel cooler and I'm much more fun

I love my family, don't get me wrong
But they're too easy to beat at ping pong!

Rudy Wilson (13)
King's Academy, Ringmer

Russia Vs Ukraine

Putin's army has attacked Ukraine.
This horrible man is completely insane.
Ukraine civilians are trying to evacuate and leave their homes.
They are hampered because there is no signal on the phones.
The men must stay behind and fight.
Women and children are forced into flight.
Volodymyr Zelensky is staying strong.
Because he knows that Putin is wrong.
Please God let this all end.

Alex Went (13)
King's Academy, Ringmer

Cars

C onfidence is key
A chieve your dreams
R esearch and become better
S earch for other ways around

F ollow your dreams
O pportunities are everywhere
R efind the right path

L ook forward not back
I nfluenced by others
F ind your happy place
E ncourage others to join the journey.

Joshua Marchant (14)
King's Academy, Ringmer

Everday Life

Everyday life is a pain,
And it is always in vain.
Love, hate, all the same,
Hurting your brain.

But maybe the cloud will pass,
It's never too late to change.
Life is like riding a bike,
Just keep moving, and you'll succeed.

Never let the storm settle,
Never let the pain sink in,
Always keep on going,
And hope will follow.

Finlay Shaw (12)
King's Academy, Ringmer

Reality

Reality
Every day they sit
The same people
Same routine
However much deeper
Is different
What lies beneath
Is shattered
Tired of repetition
Overwhelmed student
Every day
The tired teen wishes
Everything would just stop
Even for just a second
Then there would be peace
Reality
Is it always
What it seems?

Maisey Dodd
King's Academy, Ringmer

The Beautiful Game

Football, what a great game
You score and scream
Have a great time
Then when one of you is down
You help in no time
You start with a warm up
So we can build up
All the courage you have
To beat that team
To leave in gleam
Scoring top bins
Having a laugh
But that's where it begins
Having all but a headstart.

Abi Teague (11)
King's Academy, Ringmer

My Ambition

My ambition is to become an artist
But the only way I can achieve my goal is if I practise
Achieving your goal is like climbing a mountain
Making your way to get to your ambition
It's a great achievement getting to your goal
So keep trying to reach your goal
Keep trying to reach your ambitions
And keep trying to reach your dreams.

Hannah Price (12)
King's Academy, Ringmer

A Road To Disaster

We're headed for disaster;
the climate is changing faster.
We're going to have to manage,
if we're going to repair the damage.
We've got to stop pollution;
it's not the solution.
We should stop dropping litter
because it's making the world bitter.
It destroys nature
and we can't fix it later!

Jessica Standen (12)
King's Academy, Ringmer

Feeling Empowered

Feeling confident
Feeling brave enough to raise your hand
Feeling like you've got it in the bag
Feeling so encouraged that you could do anything
Feeling like all your friends have faith in you
Feeling fearless
Feeling proud of your achievements
Feeling as if today will be the best day of your life
Feeling empowered.

Gabriella Rossi (12)
King's Academy, Ringmer

The Rhythm Of War

The earth starts shaking and buildings start breaking
Fire starts flaming and people start screaming
Bombs start exploding and artillery starts firing
Sirens start beeping and children start weeping
Sargeants start shouting and soldiers start saluting
Survivors start running and the enemy starts chasing
This is the rhythm of war.

Rory Lynch (12)
King's Academy, Ringmer

Happy Must Help

There is no point in life if you are not happy
It doesn't matter if you're happy or wacky
You must take what you need
Don't forget to drop your greed
You may make your own path
But make it smooth not rude
You must see things from other people's view
Because there are many differences between me and you.

Lloyd Thomas (12)
King's Academy, Ringmer

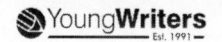

When My Body Was Mine

Staring in the mirror
Clumpy, cakey make-up drowning my face
Like all the girls at school do
I'm ugly
Still ugly
Why?
I did what I was supposed to
I know
Maybe the mirror grabs my face and distorts it
And my body
And my hair
I'll never be as pretty as them
Never
Ever
Ever.

Poppy Taranczuk
King's Academy, Ringmer

Resilience

Yes, she's been broken down.
Messed around.
Taken to the heights,
And dropped down.

But,
She's picked herself up,
Put the pieces together,
Brushed away your dirt and emerged
Stronger again.
She may have lost a move,
But not the game. And now,
Resilience is her middle name!

Jessica Frizzell (12)
King's Academy, Ringmer

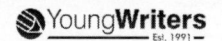

Fish And Frogs

They glisten like the sun and shine like the moon,
Their silver skin sparkles like a polished spoon.
The fish dance in the bubbles,
Whilst the frogs make trouble.
My frogs are as mischievous as can be,
But they are happiest chilling in the weeds.
They are free to roam,
I make them feel nice at home.

Elliott Luscombe (12)
King's Academy, Ringmer

No Way Back

I went to the park
I saw my favourite lark
It flew in the air where trees once stood
But now I look
There are houses as big as planes
Paths as big as lanes
If I had the power
I would empower
The people to grow instead of cutting down trees
Then we would see more leaves.

Callum Rickard (12)
King's Academy, Ringmer

My Rugby Dream

Pass with class
Collect respect
Wicked on the wing
Bewitch on the pitch
Score and want more
Attack and track back
Defend to the end
Be a sport, give support
Practise and practise

Live the dream
And play because
You love your team.

Ollie Smith (12)
King's Academy, Ringmer

My Dog Coco

My dog Coco is like an eagle
She never gives up
She is playful and always ends in cheer
I miss her when I'm at school
Coco likes to sleep
Amazing at football
My dog Coco is always into mischief
Always makes a mess with lots of biting
My dog Coco.

Isaac Parker (12)
King's Academy, Ringmer

Grampus

Grampus is as fast as a cheetah
Grampus is as big as an elephant
Grampus is as tall as a skyscraper

Quickly, quickly

Grampus is as blue as a dolphin
Grampus is as clean as a diamond
Grampus is as shiny as the sea

Quickly, quickly.

Ben Griffin (12)
King's Academy, Ringmer

She's Just Rude - Or Is She?

Look at that girl, walking over there,
Look at that girl with the brown and beautiful hair,
Let's go over and get on her case,
Yet they didn't know what she really faced.

Her brother would randomly flare up in rage,
Leaving her and those around her in fear and encaged,
She recently lost her job due to a rude boss and mates,
And this made her start losing it at an increasing rate.

They went over and messed with her hair,
Pushed her over and touched her here and there,
The girl swore and told them to leave her alone,
So they called her rude as they walked off on their own.

"It was just some unharmful banter," they assumed,
"And anyway it'll be forgotten with laughter," they presumed,
What they didn't realise was how many lives they've affected,
And how this girl's life and world were just disconnected.

So, let's not look at the girl over there,
And let's not look at the beautiful brown hair,
Because you really do not know what's going on inside,
And your further actions may make this person's mental health collide.

Rebecca Sonusi (14)
Nunnery Wood High School, Worcester

Don't Let Them Stare

Society is obsessed
With the way that I dress
Because no matter what I wear
They always stare
If I show my shoulders,
My stomach,
My legs
Or tie my hair,
I'll distract the men.
And if I wear something fancy, something nice
They ask me who I'm trying to impress,
Who I'm dressing myself up for
But if I wear something else
They tell me I don't put an effort in my appearance,
Because how I look determines my value more than my actions,
My personality,
My opinions,
They don't matter if I'm not pretty.
And God forbid that I wear revealing clothes
Because you know what men are like,
I can't risk anything.
Being raped,
Abducted,
Catcalled,
Kidnapped,

Assaulted
But if it were to happen,
It's my fault
I should've been more cautious
I shouldn't have worn that shirt
I shouldn't have worn that skirt
I should've covered up.
It's my fault that he couldn't help himself
To the sight of a young girl in a dress.
But what if things were to change?
What if I could wear what I wanted
People didn't stare,
Judge me,
Sexualise me,
They just let me wear what I felt comfortable wearing?
If we could all wear what we wanted
What makes us feel great, powerful,
What makes us different from everyone else
What makes us unique?
What if clothing wasn't gendered,
And girls could be masculine,
And boys could be feminine?
Or there was the option,
To be androgynous,
And not a single soul would stare

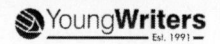

Nobody would care
Because it's your body and your choice
Not someone else's.

Julia Pieczara (14)
Nunnery Wood High School, Worcester

Empowered

Plastic is useful but it does not break down,
It spends years and years just lying around,
It litters our beaches and pollutes our seas,
We need to stop using it can you help me please!

Our oceans are full of such beautiful life
But plastic encountered causes it strife,
It wraps around their necks, their tails and their fins,
If the animals die, then no one wins,
If we use less plastic then there is less in the sea,
So please please please think of this rhyme,
When you do your shopping and pick up plastic wrapping around your limes.

It's not up to us, the young people of this world,
The older generations are the most likely to be heard,
So why can't we work together,
As a community we can send out a letter,
Send it all over the seas,
We won't stop till everyone agrees.

Can't we all find the strength to participate,
Our dream future world still awaits.
I'm writing this poem to inspire, encourage and empower you
To look from my point of view.

Izzie Faull (12)
Nunnery Wood High School, Worcester

Our Earth

Nature is what we see,
Animals living all around us,
What great sights we see,
What we have been able to feel,
Happiness, joy, satisfaction,
The love we have created with animals,
To be able to share feelings,
To be able to live alongside each other,

But what variations are being seen,
How far a body can be carried from shore,
How hot the summer can be,
How habitats are being destroyed,
How sea level is rising,
How animals are feeling these differences,
How the Earth is changing at our feet,

Species being lost,
Being endangered,
Never to be seen again,
Forgotten,
Death, destruction, despair,
Your life being changed,
With no warning,
No preparation,

You can help stop this,
You can change,
Your actions can stop this,
Stop this destruction,
Stop this sadness,
Help the animals living around you,

Change your actions,
Use renewable energy,
Be more sustainable,
Stop cutting down trees,
Only use cars for long travels or for essentials,
Only buy what you need,

If you change your actions,
You could stop what devastating things are happening around the globe,
You could be the hero,
You could be part of a great group,
Who save the environment.

Josh Ruane (14)
Nunnery Wood High School, Worcester

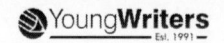

I Will Be Some Day

Sometimes the thoughts provoke a flood,
where I feel like I'm out for my own blood.
Where I feel so close to death,
that nothing can save me, not even my breath.
Where I finally crack,
underneath the stack,
of my heavy, drowning lungs.

Or sometimes there are droughts,
where I'm nothing but numb.
A bug under my own thumb.
An irritation,
an obligation,
an undeniable invitation to guilt.
But sometimes the impulsivity reigns,
where I can try to refrain,
but the tics invade my brain.
Like the tick of a clock,
the boom and the aftershock,
the crash when I finally hit bedrock.
When I tic,
it's like a building brick,
a stepping stool,
to make me look like a fool.
And people watch on and drool,
At the girl who's running out of fuel.

Sometimes I realise and open my war-torn eyes,
it's like I'm finally hearing my own cries.
I take a glass and magnify,
the feelings that fortify,
the fact that I'm not okay,
But I will be some day...

Isabelle Mann (14)
Nunnery Wood High School, Worcester

The Power Of Seven

Born on a rainy day, his creators wanted him dead
Against all wills came the starlit boy
Born with magic in his legs
Who knew he would be a wild beast?
Year after year the magic increased
One day in school a fatality happened
He threw a chair which got flattened
He knew he was born to succeed
To power other people without greed
He put up his fight and never accepted defeat
He wanted to change the world and he did with his deeds
He set an example to walk and lead
He had love, compassion and empathy instead of hiding his fears
He chose love for his fans instead of weed
No one will forget or will he perceive
One of the talented players
And never will he get defeated
Never will he give up
Never will he quit
He will be remembered for all of his good deeds
Let him be the role model we all perceive
He is the best, the great CR7
Never will we stop dreaming of being like him
But when your fantasies become your legacy
Promise him a place.

Dhyan Krishna Binu (12)
Nunnery Wood High School, Worcester

Believe Me

As the lights began to flicker
I felt as if the stage was getting bigger.
Gripping onto the jet-black mike
I felt like I was about to start a fight.
As the words came out
I knew this was the day,
And everyone around could hear
My final cheer.

"The icebergs are melting
You all must feel something."
My palms were filled with sweat
As my eyes met
With people over their heads.

Filled with anger
I have never felt any sadder,
As I felt I was the most neglected on there.
Surely someone cared
That we are soon only to breathe unhealthy air.

Turning to my left
All I could do was bet
How many people around me
Knew how this would come to be.
Eventually I will be free of the TV,
And eventually someone will believe me.

Sarah Goodman (13)
Nunnery Wood High School, Worcester

Are Animals Better Than Humans?

I saw elephants huddling around their calf
Frantically stomping to ward off predators
I saw a lion attacking a threat
To save his pride and protect his pack

I saw a dog risking his life for his owner
Willing to do anything for his approval
I saw lemurs pulling a bird out of the marsh
Even if the consequences would be harsh

But I saw a woman leaving her daughter
Because she can't be bothered to support her
I saw a man killing his friend
But it was only for a bet

Then I saw them pushing a kid
Stealing all his money
I saw a man hit his wife
All because she wanted something to eat

We do everything for money, glory and fame
We destroy our planet for one more trip to Spain
We kill for the fun of it and for our pockets

So if you were to ask me the question
Are animals better than humans?

I think I know my answer
But do you?

Amy Farrow (14)
Nunnery Wood High School, Worcester

Your Decision

Should my lips, my eyes,
My legs, be perfect to your ideas?
Does my appearance offend
Your proposal of me?

Am I my own bones, blood
Flesh? Or am I just a reflection
Of your resolve?

Does what I wear really define
Who I am, my status, my class,
My orientation, which offends your livelihood
Of 'peace and prosperity'?

Would you like me to be shorter?
Taller? Fatter? Thinner? Would you
Like me to be quiet?
Or are your prejudices
Just a constitutional presence which
You can't change? Can you?

Is this patriarchal society too
Much for you to bear?
Oh, don't worry I would like
To be that way, but maybe I can't
And why should I listen?

Would like you me to fit
Into your mould, your cage of pure
Idiocy and regret, I don't want to be
That way. Or is everything I do your decision?

Alfie Thompson (14)
Nunnery Wood High School, Worcester

Diversity

We are all the same
No matter our race, gender, or class
We should all stand as one
Because we can easily shatter like glass

We are all the same
Whether we're poor or wealthy
Because none of that should matter
As long as we're all together and healthy

We are all the same
Your race does not define you
Because we're all the same deep inside
And we're stuck like that with glue

We are all the same
Despite our gender identity
Because with a pay gap and different opinions
People get the wrong idea mentally

But we are not all the same
And we never will be
Because being different keeps us unique
And that's diversity

We can respect one another
Without bringing others down

We should all feel empowered from within
And help each other float, not drown.

Emily Kirkland (14)
Nunnery Wood High School, Worcester

You're Enough

Waking up it's hard to bear
The feeling like nobody cares
You stand slouched upon your feet
But feel a strong whiff of defeat
And though the sun shines bright
You feel like you're just in a fight
To fake a smile each and every day
And make people think you're completely okay
When really you just feel down
And feel like nobody else is around
But that group of people who are always there
Even when you think nobody cares
They guide you where you've been before
A place you didn't think was anything anymore
Happiness, light, empowerment
A place that makes you smile
That makes you want to go on every day
And feel like you'll be okay
Even though life is tough
They make you feel like you're enough.

Tia Agyemam (13)
Nunnery Wood High School, Worcester

Equality Is All We Need

Equality is all we need
Equality is all we need
To help others, to help yourself
Because you're in a wheelchair doesn't mean you're different
It doesn't matter if you are a different skin tone
Gay people shouldn't have to fight for the right to live happily
Just because there is a flag waving and dancing in the wind
Doesn't mean you can be rude
If they believe in Buddha or Brahma or Jesus
Doesn't mean you can treat them differently
Just because they're older or they're younger
Doesn't mean they can't join your game
Just because their disability isn't visible
Doesn't mean they're fake
Just because you don't like them
Doesn't mean you can't try
Equality is powerful.

Amy Evans (12)
Nunnery Wood High School, Worcester

Why...

Why do we exist?
Why do billions of others live and love?
Why do we question?
Why do we?

There is a point
To all this madness and chaos.
We just don't know it yet.
Then all we can do is try to complete our dreams and hopes
Because that is the meaning I choose.
Until we know, choose it.

Achieve your goals and hopes.
That's all we need to do.
If you want to be an astronaut
Do everything you can to be one.
If you want to be a zoologist
Then study as hard as you possibly can to be one.

The chains that stop you are weak.
They are created by you.
The very things stopping you were created by you.
If you truly try to become what you want to be
Then nothing can stop you.

Edward (12)
Nunnery Wood High School, Worcester

Despair

There is nothing you can do
They all hate you
They don't care

They think you are weird
And want you gone
They just stand there and laugh
And point and stare

They just don't understand
They can't be bothered to respect
They think you're a freak
One to abuse and glare

They want you to be perfect
But that can't be done
It's literally impossible
Like a fish breathing in air

But there is something they don't teach
That you're just one to admire
That everyone's different
And everyone's got a story to share

There's always something you can do
We don't hate you
We all truly care.

Amy Mills (13)
Nunnery Wood High School, Worcester

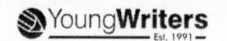

The War On Climate Change

We are blinded
Blinded like the allies
During the Blitz
Humanity is failing
This time it is no dictator
No Adolf Hitler, no Putin
No person to point our guns at

It is us
We are losing the war
The war against our climate
But going against what us humans do best
We need to help
Help the climate

And I dare speak of Hitler
Out of grief and pain
No Mussolini, no Putin
Just us to blame
Us to point our guns at
Out of cruelty and pain

But we are failing
Stuck in the trenches

With the climate charging at us
Bayonets are poised

Just like the Nazis
We are losing the war
The war against climate change
Help the climate
I dare you.

Tom Nockton (12)
Nunnery Wood High School, Worcester

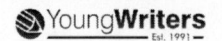

Haven

This is the place I go
When my thoughts start to grow edges
And spikes, like some new and
Frightening creature in my head.

This is the place I go
When I feel like my identity - what
Makes me, me - is wasting away
Slowly but surely.

This is the place I go
To curl up in soft bulb light and
Examine the mental wounds of the day.

This is the place I go
When sunlight and peace and love
Is devoid from the world, but
Found there, unspoiled and whole.

I know this because that
Place is *me*. It is what I stand for,
What I believe in, what and
When and why I choose to live and
Experience this beautiful world.

This is my haven.

Joe Murphy (14)
Nunnery Wood High School, Worcester

We Are Not

They want us to be strong
They want us to be brave
They want us to be perfect
They want us to be everything we're not
We're lazy, we're nervous
We're scared, we're insecure
We're jealous, we're annoyed
And we're nothing you want us to be, so stop
Stop wanting us to change, stop commenting on our lives
Stop forcing us to be this way, and stop expecting us to obey
Because some of us are different, and that's okay
Some of us are shy, some of us are confident,
Some of us are strong, some of us are smart
Some of us are loud, some of us are quiet
But either way we are all enough
Enough for ourselves
And don't need to be enough for you.

Shieanne Corpuz (13)
Nunnery Wood High School, Worcester

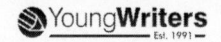

Save What We Need

The land and the sea need the same care we give each other
We need to see the bigger picture
Plastic and pollution filling our world
What are we going to do when the animals are dead and the plants won't grow?
Humans are the cause of destruction
The world needs us and we need the world
We need a change, a change of heart
Look at the positives not the negatives
Kindness is what we need, not greed
This is a real problem
If we don't solve this puzzle then we won't be looking at bright pink flowers
But flowers that are dull and dead
The weather might change, but people won't notice
The rain in summer and the sun in winter
The world won't save itself.

Alex Donello (12)
Nunnery Wood High School, Worcester

Why?

As I stare at myself in the mirror I think to myself
Why?
Why can't I look like the other girls?
Why can't I be the same?
Why don't I have a personality that can be loved and admired?
As the person in the mirror stares back at me
My eyes wander to the spots on my face, the teeth in my frown
The freckles on my cheek, my eyebrows forming a V
From the amount of time I have spent crying
My sparkling blue eyes twinkling as the light reflects into them
My full lips permanently fixed into a frown
My body perfectly proportional
As I stare into my eyes I realise being different is cool
To be unique is to be loved
If we were all the same then what's the point?

Angel Fortey (13)
Nunnery Wood High School, Worcester

How Could You?

How could you?
How could you send me home every day with tears in my eyes?
How could you change me in a month to feel nothing but betrayal?
How could you make me feel scared, anxious and angry?
How could you tear me down every day, yet you didn't even care?
You crushed me, you changed me, you destroyed me
How could you turn it around and act like it was all my fault?
I know I'm not good enough and that's because you changed me
And for that I could never forgive you
You might have changed me but you can't stop me
I will find better people
People who understand me
People who like me for who I am
And for that I thank you
Because you made me stronger.

Lara Jackson (12)
Nunnery Wood High School, Worcester

We Must Unite

They say they are doing everything
But that everything is nothing
Black blood is being shed
While innocent souls are being put in prison beds

The government is turning a blind eye to murders and crimes
If a black boy did it, he'll be serving double the time
To help clean this mess up
All of us must speak up

Tell your parents, teachers, loved ones, and everyone
Because if we all speak up it will be better than none
We can solve this issue
With all the right people

All the shades of the earth and ground
Must unite to make them understand
Please send this message to everyone you know
Together as a community we can all grow.

Kamil Kobylarz (14)
Nunnery Wood High School, Worcester

Be Yourself

Mirror, mirror on the wall
Who will really help us all?
No one, unless we do it ourselves
In this world there are no elves.
Don't be ashamed of who you are,
Embrace the inner star you are.
Go out there and show them the real you,
Don't be scared, they don't say boo.
Learn to love the skin you're in,
Be brave and don't act like a pin,
All sharp and hurtful to others,
Imagine how that would affect your mother.
Instead be kind, let that travel through your mind,
Instead be proud, don't be quiet, be loud,
Show your contagious smile,
It will surely be recorded in a file.
Be yourself,
Never let anyone change that.

Kristina Neale (12)
Nunnery Wood High School, Worcester

Believe In Yourself

Life is a road to success
It has many paths for you to proceed
Let it guide you to exceed
It will inspire you to impress
Believe in yourself!

Do not be afraid to fail
But work hard to achieve
At times you may feel quite frail
Struggle on and don't feel grief
Believe in yourself!

Drive yourself to improve
Because what is life if we have no hope
You don't ever want to disapprove
But keep going forward away from the slope
Believe in yourself!

Focus on your dreams
Always remember your intent
And your eyes will gleam
And life will keep you content
Believe in yourself!

Molly Tyrrell (14)
Nunnery Wood High School, Worcester

Fear

I want to be here, but without this fear
I wouldn't be anywhere near
My mind would be clear
I want to fit in no matter who I am
And who I want to be
I want to be here
But I sit here alone
And watch everyone else cheer
Not for me, for their children
My mum wasn't ever here
Yes, not everyone's life is perfect
And mine's certainly not near
I want to be clear
We all need to be clear
Use our voices, stand up
Push through the toughest times
Don't we all want no fear?
You stand up, make yourself clear
So everyone can hear
Let's do this together
We all want no fear.

Lacey Taylor (12)
Nunnery Wood High School, Worcester

Hopes And Dreams

Hopes and dreams, they're both the same thing
Everyone dreams every day when we all go to sleep
Everyone can dream about going to space
Or hope to get a lot of money every day
People also hope to win a raffle
While others dream about winning a game of bingo
People can dream about having one hundred dogs
When others can dream about being a celebrity
People hope racism ends
There could be a change or it could never end
People hope their family feel better
But there is still a chance it could never happen
People dream about the world getting better
There could be a chance
We could make it happen together.

James Vianello (11)
Nunnery Wood High School, Worcester

Be Yourself

You have a mind, a vision, a dream
But what if I told you it's easier than it seems?
When pushed with doubt you will persevere
And when making a choice you will choose love over fear.

When you have a thought you will speak
And you will for those who cannot or are weak
If someone was being bullied what would you do?
If you made the right choice, God will be with you

When someone helps you out you feel like you're freed
All just because they did one good deed
So go out today help lots of people
And don't just leave the people that are feeble

Be yourself.

Jack Tomboline (11)
Nunnery Wood High School, Worcester

Who Are You?

What are your limits?
The end of the train track,
The thing that defines who you are
And everything you will ever be,
Or is that just what you believe?

What is it that makes you think
You can never step beyond that line you draw
And break the cell made by you, for you?

Because it doesn't exist.
The chains, the cell, the lines you draw
Do not define you
Because nobody can define you
Not even you.

There's too much to you to define you.
No limits to stop you
Or a single person with the power to break you (just shake you).

Nathan Rhodes (12)
Nunnery Wood High School, Worcester

Believe

Believe in yourself
Open the door and try new things
Walk down the corridor of life confidently
Meet every opportunity with a smile
Believe in yourself
Follow your dreams and ambitions
Find the fire inside you
Break the boundaries and walk proudly
Believe in yourself
Unlock the gates to your future
Crawl, climb and leap through difficulties
Drive on and never stop trying
Believe in yourself
Don't fall victim to stereotypes
Fight them with your courage
Be motivated by your actions and dreams
Believe in yourself.

Harry Bloss (12)
Nunnery Wood High School, Worcester

Determined To Be The Best

You are you, you are never going to be someone else
So stop worrying about others and focus on yourself
Think positive and work really hard
So when you walk into a room
Everyone knows who you are
Mentality is key, so have some confidence
Because you might not know this
But you will be the next inspirational prodigy
Stay motivated, be determined,
Because you will be the best
And soon everyone will know this
Be humble, stay confident not cocky
Work hard in the silence
As your success will make the noise if you follow your guidance.

Jack Edwards (12)
Nunnery Wood High School, Worcester

How Nice Would Our World Be?

How nice would our world be
If we all stood for equal rights
Our world could be this nice if we all tried
No ifs, buts or mights
We could all get this if we tried

How nice would our world be
If men and women were equal
Young boys were able to play netball
Young girls were able to play rugby

How nice would our world be
If everyone were treated equally
Boys didn't have to be strong like a lion
Girls weren't thought to be weak like flies

How nice would our world be
If we all stood for equal rights.

Ruby Scarrott (13)
Nunnery Wood High School, Worcester

Do You See It?

Do you see it?
The hate, the racism
Or are you just sitting here
Letting it all happen?

Do you see it?
The people who are changing you
Messing with you
Keeping you locked away from your feelings.

Do you see it?
Them telling you
You can't be your own sexuality, religion
The way you look, the way you act.

Do they see it?
Does everyone see it?
No, they don't see it because they never will
Unless you step up and make a change
Put them in their place
Change the world for others.

Lilly Humphries (12)
Nunnery Wood High School, Worcester

Don't Have To Change

Why's my hair like that?
Why are my eyes that colour?
Why is my face like that?
Why am I not like her, her or her?

What if I dye my hair?
What if I wear contact lenses?
What if I learn how to walk differently?
What if I wear lots of make-up?
Why am I still not like her, her or her?

No... everyone is amazing in their own way
You don't have to change what you do or look like
Everyone has something special that makes them them
You don't have to change what you do or look like
Just be you.

Jess Holmes (13)
Nunnery Wood High School, Worcester

Courage

The way you love
Passionate and all-encompassing
Is not something to be ashamed of.

If they could not handle your passion
If they were scared by it
If they now make you feel guilty
For loving them too much
Don't you dare allow them
To make you doubt the courage
You carry like the sea in your soul.

You are not too emotional or weak.
Your courage is determined
By the room in your heart
To love over and over again,
Despite having it broken
By so many who were unworthy of you.

Maia Pop (13)
Nunnery Wood High School, Worcester

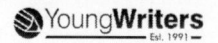

Environment

The environment, global warming
It's all crumbling, animals are dying
The world is changing
So should you, plant the seeds, stop the pollution
Help the animals and the Earth
Listen to my pleas so the world won't weep
All the hard work gone in a second
If we don't help now, no one will
And this will happen to our beautiful Earth
If we don't do this, why call it our home?
When it won't be here in fifty years
We can help this, it's our last chance
Then the world will be free at last.

Dan Turculet (12)
Nunnery Wood High School, Worcester

Education Matters

Do you want life
To be as free as a kite?
It's easier than it seems
Just join a school
It would be really cool
And if you don't
I promise you it will cost
Your education matters.

What everyone says
About school
Is just their opinion
Not yours
So join a school
Your education matters.

I know you don't want to go
But it will affect you
When you have a career
You will have no degree
So I promise you
It will cost
Your education matters.

Zoya Ali (12)
Nunnery Wood High School, Worcester

Speak Up

Many children feel afraid
Feel afraid to get the help they need
Mental illness takes control and takes away their pride
Children are afraid to speak up
And it seems fine on the outside
To others, nothing's wrong
But to some it's overwhelming
Simple tasks are made much harder
And simpler conversations can feel impossible
But all of this can be put to an end
If we all speak up, talk about our issues
Instead of hiding them
Everything will feel much better
If you speak up.

Kaiden Godding (13)
Nunnery Wood High School, Worcester

Down And Up

We come from a world where everyone is judged
We feel like we can't say a word
We want to be everyone else

We feel insecure about everything
We think to ourselves *no one likes me*
This only happens because we don't speak
Take a breath
Scream and let it all out

We come from a world where everyone is judged
No one should change for anyone else
We can be whatever we want to be
Don't let anyone bring you down
Be the one to bring everyone up.

Maroosh Akhtar (11)
Nunnery Wood High School, Worcester

The Other Side

We can't sit here and act like everything's alright
Because deep in our hearts we know it's not
Deep in our guts we know it's not
Deep in our souls we know it's not
So can you please stand with me
Walk with me
Sit with me
To show the people in power
That we are here with our minds blazing full of ideas
Full of ideas ready to preach
To teach
To educate the people who don't know the better way of life
The other side
The side without pollution.

Oliver Cartwright (12)
Nunnery Wood High School, Worcester

Beauty Standards

Acceptance
Something no one gives
If you don't look just like them
You have no reason to live
Looks
They say it's not enough
You have to be graceful while looking tough
Blind
But it only takes one to see
You don't have to be pink and perfect to be pretty
Models
They lie right to your face
You are perfect as you are without a size 0 waist
Standards
We will tear the walls down
Because everyone is gorgeous and a queen deserves her crown.

Evangeline Dowtin (13)
Nunnery Wood High School, Worcester

Powerful Citizens

As powerful as the Prime Minister or President maybe
They will never be as powerful as we
Make sure everybody has freedom
If not, help free them

We have a right to vote
If you think not, take a note
The people and citizens need power
If we don't get it, we'll seize it by the hour

Everyone deserves equality
Whether that's skin, race or ethnicity
So please do everyone a favour
And we shall all spread the word sooner or later.

Lucas Sones (12)
Nunnery Wood High School, Worcester

The Environment

The environment, it's a wonderful thing
It's the reason I can look out of my window
And see birds singing, flowers blooming and blue skies
However, this beauty is quickly diminishing before me
Meaning I get to view birds dying, flowers shrivelling and grey skies all around
But we can change this
We can stop the environmental genocide we are rapidly causing
Our time on this planet is fleeting
Without action we will soon discover
The fatal consequences.

Matthew Blaikie (14)
Nunnery Wood High School, Worcester

Make The Change

Want to take a risk, make a change
Struggling to deal with all the pain
Want something to change for yourself
And all the people who helped you get through the rain
Don't wait for something to happen to come your way
Go and chase it, whatever it takes
Don't be the one to stand still,
Fake a smile and say it's all okay
Because everyone goes through bad times
And their ups and downs
Because eventually everyone makes it to the good side.

Maliakah Arshad-Mehmood (13)
Nunnery Wood High School, Worcester

Nature Is Around Us

Flower petals
And forest green
Come together in the world we see
Earth goes by day by day
Will humans ever pay?

From the leaves in the tree
To the air that we breathe
Nature is around us
Day and night, day and night
The ocean blue
Creates a view
That is priceless

Pollution is killing
The trees, leaves and bees
We won't have these views
Or the forest green
Unless we help to keep our world clean.

Tom Brown (14)
Nunnery Wood High School, Worcester

Help

People like Marcus change the world
People like Marcus change people's minds
People like Marcus help people in need
Help Marcus Rashford

Change your views and comments
Help others change their thoughts
Help Marcus change the world
Help Marcus Rashford

People like Marcus help the environment
People like Marcus change the world
Help Marcus Rashford
Make the world a better place
Put a smile on someone's face.

Dion Cartwright (13)
Nunnery Wood High School, Worcester

Poems

Poems, we have all read them
They make us dream of success
They inspire us to do great things
Those great things make us believe
Believing we can be great
Poems are very well known
Like Martin Luther King has a statue of his own
Poems can make decisions
Those decisions lead to success
Success is what people believe
Believing is the key
The key to life
Life has a key
We must open it
Unleash your greatness.

Archie Burton (12)
Nunnery Wood High School, Worcester

Confidence

Feeling lost, feeling scared, feeling weak
Be confident, be strong, be competitive
Perfect performance, perfect voice, perfect tone
I have confidence, I have trust, I believe
I smile, I speak, I finish
I don't care what people think, I am myself
I stand up for myself with my confidence and my strength
It doesn't matter what people think about you
If you're confident, stay confident
Don't change for anyone.

Summer Drummond (11)
Nunnery Wood High School, Worcester

Injustice

The injustices between humans kill to this day
After countless wars and tragedies, still we let it lay
The victims of brutality killed without reason
How do we let people murder as if it's treason?
"No justice, no peace" is screamed through the streets
Yet we allow humanity to fall apart beneath our feet
Sectors of people separated by the colour of their skin
And people still think that racism doesn't lie within.

Antoinette Thea Ragasa (13)
Nunnery Wood High School, Worcester

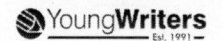

Suffer No Longer

War,
People are dying
People are hiding
Russia is dominating

The beasts are killing civilians
Forcing them to run
Millions need help
Who's there to give it?

World, listen to my pleas
Russia's treating people like fleas
Cruel cops arresting all who oppose
War isn't what Ukraine chose

Stand up for yourselves
Stand up for others
Don't let evil stop you now.

Harvey Symonds (12)
Nunnery Wood High School, Worcester

Dreams Need To Be Achieved

Who do you want to be?
What do you want to achieve?
Do you want to become a politician
And make the right decision?

Or do you want to become a hero?
But what does that mean?
Helping people, making people laugh
Or even something small
Like picking up litter
But don't pick up a filter
Be proud of who you are!

Act now to what you think is right
Or what is wrong
Time is ticking.

Ayesha Tabassum (13)
Nunnery Wood High School, Worcester

The Flow

Do you feel it?
The endless, bottomless pit of light.
That is our flow,
The flow of light
Our light
No, your light.

Do you feel it?
It's pumping through your veins
Your skin
Your lungs
Your heart!

Whatever flows through your heart,
It's you!
The love, the pain, the passion.
Don't let it go,
Let it flow!
You have your light,
You have your flow.

James Barratt (12)
Nunnery Wood High School, Worcester

The Environment

Roses are red, violets are blue
I want to keep the environment true

Increased temperatures from global warming
And we've already been given a warning
Forests burn and animals live
And we stand and watch as they die

Plastic pollution and all this food waste
Just because we don't like the taste
Oceans perish and pass underwater
And we hesitate to react and watch what we slaughter.

Monty Simpson (13)
Nunnery Wood High School, Worcester

Keep Running

When the world stops spinning, keep running
When something holds you back, keep moving
When something is in your way, no excuse
When you get opportunity, take it
When you get lent a hand, shake it

When something gets you down, get back up
When you hit the bottom, climb back up
When the world changes, adapt,
When you get stuck, keep trying

When the word stops spinning, keep running.

Gracie Lee (12)
Nunnery Wood High School, Worcester

Equality

Equal rights are equal power
Even when it feels quite sour
Who are you and what am I?
Questions that we can't define

Differences are who we are
We need to push this hate so far
Overrule and overpower
It's not their world, it's ours

So do not hide from the hate
Instead stand up and join the fate
For here I stand upon this world
Waiting to spread the word.

Jessica Cattermole (11)
Nunnery Wood High School, Worcester

Food For Thought

Humans are like food
From pasta to pineapple
Bananas to bacon
Apples to avocado

We're all different
Everybody has their advantages
Somebody likes you
Somebody likes somebody else

You are liked
Maybe even loved
Like a pasta
Somebody loves you

Like an avocado
Somebody else loves somebody else
You have to find the right person
For you.

Steven Evans (14)
Nunnery Wood High School, Worcester

But Why?

But why do I act like this?
You might think
There is no answer;
You are you - stop doubting yourself.
But why?
There is no answer because you are you.
But you still doubt yourself
And hide from people, from you.
But why?
You're afraid of people.
But why?
Everyone's different;
You are different.
You are you.
Being different is normal
So be normal.

Salma Sherif (11)
Nunnery Wood High School, Worcester

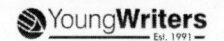

My Fault Not Theirs

If I put the effort into what I wear
I'm dressing to impress
But if I wear what I'm comfortable in
It means I don't care
My looks now define me, is that how it is?
That dress, that skirt, that hair...
What happened to my beliefs, my happiness, my feelings?
But why should any of that matter?
Because if they look over and stare
Of course it's my fault, not theirs.

Macy Holder (14)
Nunnery Wood High School, Worcester

Are You Good Enough?

Are you good enough?
Good enough to be in a world
Full of people,
Full of pressure,
Full of love.
When you try to fit in
But you can't because
You think you're not good enough.

You try to be someone you're not
To impress those who you think are perfect
But in reality
The only people you need to impress
Are those who
Love you.

Amelia Ali (12)
Nunnery Wood High School, Worcester

Bring People Together

Cancer can destroy people or bring them together
Cancer can create fear or create love
But no matter what, you can't give up
Because there's always a chance no matter what
Don't let people bring you down
Don't let problems bring you down
Because no matter what, some people will always root for you
Because to some people you mean the world.

Callum Bannister (13)
Nunnery Wood High School, Worcester

Empowered Women

Empowered women
Equality is their right
Strong, confident, brave
History shows they will put up a fight

You may know one or be one
They will always be around
Their words won't be silenced
They may often astound

Empowered women
They are a capable decision maker
Courageous and powerful
Solution finder yet risk taker.

Cerys Jones (14)
Nunnery Wood High School, Worcester

Believe You Can

Believe you can do
What you want to
If you disagree
You can see
This is the key
To the changes that
Need to be made

Believe you can use your power
Don't wait till the 11th hour
If you wait it'll be too late

Believe you can make the change
It can be big or it can be small
It doesn't matter, not at all.

Oliver Leonard (12)
Nunnery Wood High School, Worcester

I Am

Am I safe?
Am I sick?
Am I in the wrong?
Am I in trouble?
Do they like me?
Do I have the power to be strong?
Uncontrollable thoughts
Isolated from the outside
Will I escape?
I can do this
We are all different
We all face challenges
We will get through it
I can do this
Anxiety is strong
But I'm stronger.

Ben Schaus (12)
Nunnery Wood High School, Worcester

This Is Me

From the second I was born
I have been judged
From the clothes I wear
To the way I style my hair
But I don't care what you think
Or anyone for that matter
Because I am who I am
And that's all that matters
So don't try to change me
If you don't like that
Don't talk to me
Because this is my personality.

Charlie Bunce (12)
Nunnery Wood High School, Worcester

The Earth

Look around at the grass and the trees
The land and the seas
Look around at the delicate flowers
And the things that we call ours
Look around and see its beauty
We should protect it
It is our duty
Everything that has been created
Needs to be kept and appreciated
Everything that has worth
Should be cared for like the Earth.

Aleena Ilyas (14)
Nunnery Wood High School, Worcester

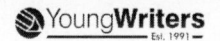

In The Dust

Those who fought are left in the dust
While those who survived leave them to rust
We became too confident, overcome with greed
And we committed a terrible deed
They gave us their lives, their happiness, their future
And yet we just left them in the dust
So now we must atone for our sins
And remember them always
As those who never left.

Sam Jennings (12)
Nunnery Wood High School, Worcester

Dreams And Wishes

All of our dreams
Our hopes
And our wishes
Can come true
If we try to make
Them come true
But no matter
What happens
You will have
That power
You need
To do that
So just
Try to
Even if
You think
You're failing just
Keep trying
You'll get there
Eventually.

Georgia Grooms (11)
Nunnery Wood High School, Worcester

Equality

Love who you are
No matter the scar
Colour, love, disability
No matter your sexuality

Love who you are
No matter where you are
Equality is love
Love is grace
No matter your race

Love who you are
Everyone is unique
Remember equality
And make it a good place.

Evie Kirkland (12)
Nunnery Wood High School, Worcester

Life And Rights

Fight for a right
Speak out loud with no fear
We are here to stop treason
People live and die for a reason

Everybody makes bad decisions in life
But you can always make them right
People like Putin, Hitler and terrorists were all wrong
We need to stand and fight for our rights.

Lincoln Atkins (12)
Nunnery Wood High School, Worcester

Confidence

Be confident
You need to be confident to succeed
You are you
You will never be anyone else
Be optimistic
Stop focusing on the negatives
Start focusing on the positives
Be determined
Be the one who leads
Never stop your beliefs because of someone else.

Harry Davies (13)
Nunnery Wood High School, Worcester

Identity

Identity is what makes me
It makes me feel as if I can be myself
I laugh
I smile
But sometimes I can do a mile
I may seem shy
I may seem boring
But I can try what I want to try
I can be happy
I can be sad
But sometimes I can go mad.

Tanisha Parrott (12)
Nunnery Wood High School, Worcester

Make A Change

The world is falling apart
If no one speaks up who will?
The time is right to make a change
Before the world crumples again

What future will we have
If no one wants to help?
We need someone to make a start
So others can begin to follow.

Thomas Walters (13)
Nunnery Wood High School, Worcester

Belief

Belief is a power,
Belief is a strength,
Belief is hope,
Belief can bring unity,
Belief can bring peace,
Belief is the light in one's darkness,
Belief is a guide for those who are lost,
Belief is something that brings people together.

Siddhant Dubey (13)
Nunnery Wood High School, Worcester

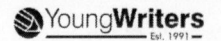

Be Strong

Believe in yourself
Be confident
Be strong
It's time to be wrong
Everyone makes mistakes
Dream big
Be empowered
Be happy
You have an opportunity
In this community
So go out there
And find what's easy for you.

Mikayeel Akbar (12)
Nunnery Wood High School, Worcester

Hopes, Dreams And Ambitions

A distant memory
A growing ambition
Is this all a superstition
Blinded by money
The issues no longer funny
Ambitions falter away
All goes astray
Joy at bay
What will you do now?

Thea Fieldhouse (12)
Nunnery Wood High School, Worcester

Ukraine

Feeling sorry for our loved ones
Family and friends
Checking up on them daily
To make sure they're still okay
Silence is a bad thing
Always wanting my phone to ring.

Emily Franklin (12)
Nunnery Wood High School, Worcester

No Perfect Body

Just remember,
There is no perfect body.

No perfect height, no perfect shoe size,
No perfect anything.
An hourglass figure is not perfect.
Whether you have a tiny waist or none at all,
You are beautiful.
No eye colours are perfect either.
Yes there are rare ones, but not perfect ones.
There is no such thing as a perfect face shape,
No jawline or face structure is any better than the other.
Whether you have a round face, square face, diamond face,
It doesn't matter.

Because you are beautiful.

Anyway, it doesn't matter about the outside,
What defines your beauty is the inside…
But still,
Just remember,
There is no perfect body.

Anya Wood
RGS Worcester, Upper Tything

Darkness

The doorbell goes
Just the mailman
Newspapers full of horror and despair
Like dagger knives hit my heart
Flicking through
The words turn grey with the trauma that fills my heart

I stop to crawl inside the cupboard
The place I saw my parents fall
The things I'd do to see them again
But now this is normal
Stay here until the end is here
But

The bridge is close
There's nothing left to live
Everywhere I go is death and destruction
Everywhere is dark
The hope is gone
And so my spark inside has gone.

Issy Pottinger (13)
RGS Worcester, Upper Tything

Looks

Looks...
Or the bland characteristics we occasionally find in books.
We idolise the fake...
And this introspection we must take.
These brands
These cosmetics
All so pathetic
They deceive us for their greed
More and more wealth they seem to need
People's wages are depleting
These 'powers' we aren't defeating
They trick us all with sponsorships and size
When they try to mask their lies
Perfection can't be achieved
So until then
We will continue to be
Ourselves.

Eva Wilson-Thomas (12)
RGS Worcester, Upper Tything

I Am Only 13

I am only 13,
Trapped in my thoughts,
Finding myself alone every day,
Not seeing my family.
Lockdown steals the friends I have.
I feel imprisoned.

Laptop lessons are not the same.
I thought this was going to be fun,
But it's just boring and lame.
I am only 13.

People dying,
Shots getting louder.
Screaming, "I can't breathe!"
All this arguing makes me tried,
These police officers need to be fired!
Why can't they understand?
Black lives matter and it's getting out of hand.
Children getting shot in the knee,
Why do they seem as young as me?

Something's on the news.
World War Three?
How can we survive this catastrophe?
So many disasters happening, surrounding me,
What is going to happen to the older me?

Daisy Hossack (13)
St Andrew The Apostle School, London

The Voices

The pencil is not in the right place,
The voices in my head running in a race,
"Turn the pencil to the left",
My life is being taken away like a theft.

My fist tightens whilst looking at my bed,
The voices repeating in my head,
"Make the bed three times",
"Turn the pillow around."

"You will get in a car crash",
The ominous warnings rage in a flash,
They tell me I will die,
Doing these things are making me cry.

I wake up, brush my teeth,
Wondering if these voices will give me grief.
I rinse my mouth, dry my face,
Head spinning all over the place.

I brace myself for what is to appear,
The voices seem to slowly disappear,
I shriek with joy, although to my despair,
Some voices seem to still be there.

Christiana Christofi (12)
St Andrew The Apostle School, London

Women In Sport

Women are as capable as men,
It is wrong to be discriminating against them!
Women can play any sport.

They can play football,
And volleyball,
They can play anything and everything,
'Cause they are something.

They are skilled
And have talent.
Have you heard of Alex Morgan?
One of the best footballers?

Dina-Asher Smith,
One of the greatest runners,
And will always be,
She wins most of her races.
Serena Williams,
You must have heard of her?
A great tennis player.
There is no motivation like her.

Every female can play sports,
So here are many lessons that can be taught.
Females can achieve anything they want to achieve,
They just need to be strong and to just believe.

Katina Georgiou
St Andrew The Apostle School, London

Lockdown

Seconds, minutes, days, weeks, crawled by.
Our lives felt like a black hole,
The eerie silence followed me,
Constantly sitting there, with rotten breath,
I longed for this to be over.

All laughter drained out of you.
Shrouded in complete darkness.
With nowhere else to go,
Confined, locked, and shut away from reality.
Sitting there at a computer screen,
What does this all mean?
But finally, there was something keen.
There was a gleam, and there was a beam.

Finally, the silence escaped me.
I could now see
And smiles surrounded me
Life was finally free.

Michael Georgiou (12)
St Andrew The Apostle School, London

Tick Tock

Tick tock,
Tick tock,
Sounds the clock.
Time goes by slowly, but it does not stop.

Tick tock,
Tick tock,
I pray to God,
Whilst the screaming knocks.

Tick tock,
Tick tock,
I wonder what has happened to the country I've lost.

Tick tock,
Tick tock,
My heart drops, like the bombs from above.

Tick tock,
Tick tock,
In the back of my mind, as a gun goes off.

Tick tock,
Life will soon stop.

So, when you read this poem,
Please think of me,
When you live in your world of safety, so happily.

Ana Halliday
St Andrew The Apostle School, London

Captured And Locked Away

Locked away,
Locked away,
Oh, how wrong it is for me.
Hair in knots and smiles like bolts,
Dreams so green,
But the world is a black, gleaming beam.

I feel like I'm drowning,
I feel like I'm sinking
If only someone pulled me,
Out and away from,
This lonely abyss of feeling.

I've learnt a lot now,
I've learnt how to cope.
One call of the day could,
Save the damsel in many a way.

Sitting down with a cup in my hand,
Sitting and talking.
Oh, how I wished I had done this sooner.

Sahana Goonasekera
St Andrew The Apostle School, London

Lonely Isolation

Time slows down,
Minutes into hours,
Hours into days.
It comes over me,
Grey around me,
Loneliness engulfs me.

Day in, day out,
For eternity trapped,
Never, never again,
No sleep, no hope,
Trapped in a case of loneliness.

Testing day by day,
Testing, alarmed at being positive,
I will never leave,
I am forced to stay.

I can break free,
I can socialise,
I can run free
I can stop being lonely.

Stefan Kousoulou
St Andrew The Apostle School, London

Dear Future Self

Dear future self, you will not be tamed
Dear future hero, I'm proud of your scars
Dear future lion, your roar has woken.

Dear future self, fly to fail
Dear future hero, never fail to fly
Dear future lion, no one can ever deafen your inner roar
It just becomes louder.

Dear future self, you are the future
Dear future hero, you were born for a reason
Dear future lion, roar without apology.

Dear future self, hard work is your swollen success
Dear future hero, success is your revenge
Dear future lion, earn your respect.

Dear future self you are the problem
Dear future hero, you are the change
Dear future lion, all want the honour but few hunt for it.

Dear future self, you can do it.
Dear future hero, you will do it.
Dear future lion, you must.

Dear future self, don't underestimate your power.
Dear future hero, listen to me, your 'present' hero.
Dear lion, ROAR...!

Jeremiel Mbogol (12)
Trinity Academy Leeds, Leeds

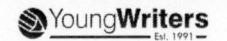

Sadness Of A Crybaby

The sadness of a crybaby is
Deep and dull. A constant
Stabbing from the chest
Causing tears to
Fall down rapidly
Causing us crybabies
To ride them.

The sadness of a crybaby is
Cold and sadly lonely.
It has
No one to love them
No one to call 'friend'
They die in the shadows waiting
And waiting
But no one arrives.

The sadness of a crybaby
Is silent and soft.
Their calmness fading into
Anger and hatred, fuming
Like a volcano to erupt.

The sadness of a crybaby
Is annoying and loud.
They cry out loud letting
Out all of the painful words

Sink and disappear into
Our ears. But not even those
Tears which form floods
Can wipe away all existence but it's still
Not enough to stop the angry, fearful
Words to wander around in her head.

The sadness of a crybaby is
Smiling and happy
The smile is bright and bold.
So bright that the sun couldn't compare.
She could smile and that's what I'm after.
The smile in her eyes.
The sound of hereafter.

Moram Osman (12)
Trinity Academy Leeds, Leeds

My Thoughts Out Loud

I always wonder who am I meant to be,
What can I achieve and what do I believe.
I as a person have lots of insecurities
about how I should look and what should I eat.

All around me I see these 'perfect beauties'
Who are fit to be models and act like queens.
Most times I compare myself with them to see if I'm of quality,
But end up feeling a pang of jealousy that makes me feel empty.

But I always seem to remember that I'm beautiful just the way I am,
and that I shouldn't compare myself to those who, deep down, are probably suffering;
both mentally and physically.
Instead, I should be encouraging others who are finding it difficult to express how they feel,
both male female and remind them that they are not alone because,
I've learned that if one person fails than we all fail but,
If one succeeds then we celebrate for we have all succeeded.

To tell you the truth, I'm as lost as ever.
Whilst others have their life planned out,

I'm still wondering what I want to be,
but I now know that my thoughts are free.

Abigail Kidane (12)
Trinity Academy Leeds, Leeds

Dreams

Some are big, some are small
Some don't take any time at all
Where will your dreams take you?
For each and every one of us, it's different.
We hold onto dreams.
For if we don't, dreams wither.
Life will be like broken-winged parrot.
So beautiful, yet so damaged.
If we turn that around,
If we be tenacious enough,
Determined enough,
Strong-willed enough,
We could be anything.
We could be athletes, lawyers, doctors,
Scientists, philosophers, we could even be astronauts.
But only if we put our mind to it.
So, work towards it,
The dreams, the aspirations,
Why not pave your way to success?
Like a road
Lay one brick today, lay another tomorrow
And over time, you will notice the difference,
Success,
A dream accomplished.

Mustafa Goulami (11)
Trinity Academy Leeds, Leeds

Faithful Memories

As I began my joyful journey
I sprinted past the floral, sparsely populated field.
I noticed that it was full of many gorgeous
Brightly attracting plants.
I ran my hand across the delicate flowers.
The scented, sweet breeze of all the different flowers...
Daisies, roses, dandelions...
The faint touch of the delightful flowers brought tears to my eyes.
As my tears dropped on the glamorous green grass
Sorrowful memories came back to sight
Sorrowful memories of my long-lost family
Sorrowful memories of my long-lost friends
Sorrowful memories of my long-lost grandparents
Sorrowful memories that were never to leave my side
Sorrowful memories that were here for life till my destiny.

Tasnim Mohammed (12)
Trinity Academy Leeds, Leeds

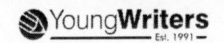

A Voice That Mattters

Why does a voice matter?
What does it do?
Why do people use it?
Does it matter to you,
So many questions,
I wish I wish I could share my answer to.

We all have opinions,
And in my opinion voices are strong,
Stronger together combined as one,
Differences shouldn't exist,
We all have a right to use one,
Some may be unique,
We shouldn't judge,
Because using your voice can be someone's dream,
To be heard for sticking up for rights they believe in,
Maybe one day using your voice can be easier,
Than not using your voice.

Laaibah Hussain (12)
Trinity Academy Leeds, Leeds

Dreams

Some are big,
Others are just small.
You've got to choose
Can't have them all.

Some come true,
Others sadly can not.
A few you remember
Most you forgot.

Some are important
Others you can live without.
For some you will have to fight,
And for others you might not.

Some last a day,
Others a lifetime.
Not only dream at night
But also during the day.

Some are possible,
Others are not,
But you have to dream on,
Sometimes it's all you've got.

Amina Almjadami (12)
Trinity Academy Leeds, Leeds

Success

As the wind waves and the tide twirls,
Standing beside me, always a group of friends.
Supporting, caring, always beside me,
Together, we take one glance at the sea.

As it glistens and gushes in patterns towards the surface,
Seeing a bright future lay before me
Seeming so perfect.

Crouching down to get a closer look,
Realising the key to success has always been in our school books
Realising our future depends on our choices of the present
Realising our actions define who we are and what it makes us.

Deyana Ismail (12)
Trinity Academy Leeds, Leeds

My Life

When I started at the new school it was not too good.
I ran out of classes, had fits.
It was the old me but now
I am learning and sit in class.
But that is at school.
At home it is harder.
I am the oldest from
five kids.
Imagine
doing all of the chores at home
with 4 kids around you.
But no one is perfect.
Not even the queen Elisabeth.
Every kid at school should work harder
so when they get their exam results
they think the work paid off.

Jaromira Stejckova (12)
Trinity Academy Leeds, Leeds

This Is Life

I face the unknown as to life does to a teen
I have not seen this globe nourish and gleam
I may not fly like a free bird in the sky
But my aspirations and dreams fly high
This is life, this is life.

Although our destination is most key
It is our journey that makes us glee
There are many thresholds and hurdles
Along the way
If there's no hard work and dedication our dreams soon decay
This is life
This is life.

Ansh Minhas (12)
Trinity Academy Leeds, Leeds

Friends

The reason why friends are important to me is because
They are the one thing you can turn to
Someone who can lift you when you feel down
It can be an animal or a person
It can be a person that resonates with you
Someone who can have your back
A person who protects you in your darkest moments
They could be in every shape and size
They will make you laugh
Because they are your
Friend.

Uali Binium (12)
Trinity Academy Leeds, Leeds

Summer

I can see the grass growing
Throughout the open window
It doesn't have to know
About multiplication
It just gets on with it
I wish it would swallow
This room: make a jungle
Where we could hunt for
Adders to help our
Maths to those
Large snakes to tell us
About Pythagoras
Theory.

Athelia Duberry (11)
Trinity Academy Leeds, Leeds

My Inspiration

I am always inspired
By the way she lives life.
Her smile of joy,
The glint in her eye.

I always admire
His commitment to find
The answers he needs
To help me survive.

They always encourage me to be great,
To work hard and live on,
And teach me success will never come too late.

Ryan Adam (12)
Trinity Academy Leeds, Leeds

Equality

E veryone is the same no matter their differences
Q uantity shouldn't matter
U nique
A ll united as a family
L ove others no matter what their gender, race, heritage or sexuality
I ncludes everyone
T ogether as a union
Y ou're all important.

Jasmine Fielding (12)
Trinity Academy Leeds, Leeds

Sunflower

Akin to a sunflower in the tundra
Beaten and bruised
By hateful hail
Grey skies once lived under

However, still standing tall

Ready to ride waves of opportunity
Still grasping onto rays of rosiness
Still striving for survival and more

Just see how high I will reach.

Nicole Bazenova (12)
Trinity Academy Leeds, Leeds

Your True Self

What matters most
Can be found in your ghost.
The sun is as bright as day
No need to leave: stay.
Every day is better with you,
No need to act blue.
Show your true self:
Come out of the bookshelf.

Chloe Elysse Carag (12)
Trinity Academy Leeds, Leeds